MICHAEL SORKIN STUDIO

OTHER
PLANS

PAMPHLET ARCHITECTURE WAS INITIATED IN 1977 AS AN INDEPENDENT VEHICLE TO CRITICIZE, QUESTION, AND EXCHANGE VIEWS. EACH ISSUE IS ASSEMBLED BY AN INDIVIDUAL AUTHOR/ARCHITECT. FOR MORE INFORMATION, PAMPHLET PROPOSALS, OR CONTRIBUTIONS PLEASE WRITE TO PAMPHLET ARCHITECTURE, C/O PRINCETON ARCHITECTURAL PRESS, 37 EAST 7TH STREET, NEW YORK, NEW YORK, 10003.

* OUT OF PRINT, AVAILABLE ONLY IN THE COLLECTION PAMPHLET ARCHITECTURE 1 THROUGH 10

MICHAEL SORKIN STUDIO
UNIVERSITY OF CHICAGO STUDIES 1998-2000

OTHER PLANS

PAMPHLET ARCHITECTURE #22

PRINCETON ARCHITECTURAL PRESS
NEW YORK

PUBLISHED BY
PRINCETON ARCHITECTURAL PRESS
37 EAST SEVENTH STREET
NEW YORK, NEW YORK 10003

FOR A FREE CATALOG OF BOOKS, CALL 1.800.722.6657.
VISIT OUR WEB SITE AT WWW.PAPRESS.COM.

PROJECT EDITOR: JENNIFER N. THOMPSON
COPY EDITOR: LINDA LEE
DESIGNER: MICHAEL SORKIN STUDIO / DAVID KONOPKA

SPECIAL THANKS TO: NETTIE ALJIAN, ANN ALTER, AMANDA
ATKINS, NICOLA BEDNAREK, JANET BEHNING, MEGAN CAREY,
PENNY CHU, JAN CIGLIANO, JANE GARVIE, TOM HUTTEN,
CLARE JACOBSON, MARK LAMSTER, NANCY EKLUND LATER,
ANNE NITSCHKE, EVAN SCHONINGER, LOTTCHEN SHIVERS,
AND DEB WOOD OF PRINCETON ARCHITECTURAL PRESS—
KEVIN C. LIPPERT, PUBLISHER

SORKIN, MICHAEL, 1948-
  PAMPHLET ARCHITECTURE 22 : OTHER PLANS : UNIVERSITY OF CHICAGO
STUDIES, 1998-2000 / BY MICHAEL SORKIN.
    P. CM.
  ISBN 1-56898-309-3 (PBK. : ALK. PAPER)
  1. UNIVERSITY OF CHICAGO—BUILDINGS—HISTORY. 2. UNIVERSITY OF
CHICAGO—PLANNING—HISTORY. I. TITLE: PAMPHLET ARCHITECTURE TWENTY-TWO.
II. UNIVERSITY OF CHICAGO. III. TITLE.
  LD931 .S67 2002
  727'.3'0977311—DC21
                                                2001004013

CONTENTS

PREFACE

The provenance of this plan is somewhat fraught. Commissioned to produce an "alternative" master plan, we had barely begun when we were perfunctorily dropped. But the campus held the studio too tightly in its grip and so we have pushed on, both out of fascination with this beautiful place and in continuing frustration at the underwrought prosody of current plans.

There is an ambiguity at the core of the university's official plan that is intrinsic to masterplanning in general: how far to go, how precisely to prescribe the architectural outcomes desired. The university has chosen to hedge its bets by adopting a predictive, functionalist plan. Based on values of consultation and consensus, the plan views architectural decisions as the the direct outcome of programmatic analysis. Not itself architectural, the plan is meant to form the armature for architecture to be added later.

This process is provisional by design, nominally flexible. Absent architecture, however, the plan lacks the means to test its own conclusions, which remain general until filled out by specifics. The master plan, itself a product of tremendous investment, cannot be altered without imperiling the many compacts embodied, even when architecture suggests otherwise. Such planning, however efficient, is only poetic by chance. Vetted mainly for agreement, there is, within the process, no aspiration to the remarkable, merely the apparently logical or reasonable.

Such a formally deductive strategy seeks creativity only as an outcome, in the hope that remarkable architecture will emerge on the sites it neutrally suggests. Because its imagination is schematic, however, the university's official plan cannot truly investigate the most critical formal issue faced by the campus: the poetics of ensemble, a comprehensive idea of place. By excluding both architectural precision and careful commitment to the character of the "negative" spaces architecture produces, vision is reduced to retrofit and luck.

The project presented here is another sort of plan, a comprehensive or "all-at-once" strategy. Henry Ives Cobb's initiating scheme for the university was such a plan, a fantasy of completion, imagined down to its architectural particulars. This mode seems especially relevant today, with the university set to transform its north and south campuses, build new complexes for the School of Business and the hospitals, and remake residential life, a combined area greater than the original quads.

The University of Chicago has long prided itself on the rigor and vitality of its self-analysis, its institutional skepticism. In the midst of a typically dramatic period of investigation and debate, a comprehensive plan can serve as an armature for reflection, not simply about the campus but the structure and purposes of the university itself. This plan, in its specificity, is offered in the hope that it can be of some service to the argument.

Michael Sorkin '69

The City White hath fled the earth
But where the azure waters lie,
A noble city hath its birth,
The City Grey that ne'er shall die.

The Cobb Plan △

THE CITY GREY

The best known image of the University of Chicago is of a place that doesn't exist: Henry Ives Cobb's famous bird's-eye view of the university's founding plan. This was Cobb's vision of the campus at formal climax, of the all-at-once, the quadrangles complete. The drawing was meant both to evoke the atmosphere that Cobb imagined for the campus and to provide a guide for its elaboration. Although the build-out of the quads doesn't exactly correspond to Cobb's initiating idea, it displays remarkable fidelity to that first fantasy.

Cobb's view is also striking for what it doesn't show. The perspectival image floats in abstraction, its context a continuous street grid, each block filled with greenery. Missing is any idea of the community beyond its walls—those unspecified surroundings could be anything. The absence is strategic, a portrait of the ivory tower, flourishing in its isolation. While such disengagement may be the matrix of scholarly endeavor—the ground of "objectivity"—it also speaks of the unworldliness of the university and of a history of ambivalent relations to its neighbors.

The originating version of such a cloistered community of scholars is, of course, the cloister, the highly ritualized monastic fellowship. Aspects of this model have great appeal: the sense of community, the quiet atmosphere of contemplation, and the historic architectures contoured to reflection and disputation. Other qualities are less attractive: the rigorous isolation from the outside world, the oppressive levels of ritual and regimentation, a certain intolerance.

The hoariest academic version of this is Oxbridge (with its own ecclesiastical roots) and a fantasy of leavened monasticism (St. Gall plus panty raids . . .) still undergirds the contemporary idea of the way a university should be. The question for campus planning is how to modify or inflect this architectural model both to fit a university's own special character and organization and to interact with the specifics of locale and milieu. Community always engages a vector of setting—context affects character. If, for example, one overlays bohemianism (a more contemporary source of campus atmosphere) on the monastic model, a different version of the dialectic of isolation and community arises. Bohemianism, a modern, urban phenomenon, proposes another style of self-isolation, the garret, another form of communion, the cafe, and another form of settlement, the anonymity of city life.

The University of Chicago faces a special challenge in balancing the claims of town and gown. Here, available models are less helpful. The classic American paradigm of the university in a small-town setting is both apt and inappropriate. Hyde Park does have many qualities of a small-town or suburb and yet, as a part of Chicago, hemmed by struggling neighborhoods, built to urban densities, it is quite different. This means that ready-made strategies, whether the Oxbridge, Cambridge, Mass., Berkeley, or Ann Arbor college town models, or the dispersed big city styles of the Sorbonne or NYU, don't really help.

Where to look for the *genius loci*? The University of Chicago campus sits at the convergence of two seminal American urban artifacts: the grid and the park. The history of the university's building frames a continuing debate about the relative importance of these elements and has, over the years, produced an inventory of strategies for dealing with them. A century of building has seen repeated shifts in attitudes, and the ongoing saga of campus growth casts these twists and turns in stone. The current breakdown of consensus about both Cobb's and subsequent styles of blending, however, requires reinvestigation and reinvention. The context, after all, has changed dramatically.

Chicago is the quintessential American metropolis and the birthplace of our architectural modernity. Virtually uninflected by topography, the city is the point of departure for the Jeffersonian gridiron that organized the western infinity. Symbol of Cartesian democracy, the grid produces a territory of nominal equality, dividing the entire country into identical increments of property. The grid manages conflicting spatial claims via a universal order sited, in theory, at a level of generalization sufficiently broad to preserve the freedom of the individual actors.

While the quads are fitted into the city gridiron, they are also inserted into the Chicago park system—the mighty legacy of the City Beautiful movement. The university is surrounded by superb parks and by the rolling vastness of Lake Michigan. Olmsted's parks, romantic, meandering, and "organic," are the formal, and in many ways conceptual, antithesis of the grid, if equally artificial. The campus is the continuation of both the grid and this green system by other means, framing a series of miniaturized versions of the great parks in its quadrangles, creating an internal archipelago of green chambers. However, while the parks participate in a naturalistic fantasy of unboundedness, as if nature were simply excerpted, the quads depend on their strong and precise figuration. If we read the parks for their continuity, we read the quadrangles for their singularity and disjunction, for their geometrical order of enclosure.

The Chicago quads differ from their Oxbridge source in that the orthogonality unremittingly exists in Chicago while the English examples—wiggled by topography, river, and a medieval urbanism that had yet to rediscover the grid—have a more organic, informal flavor that adds a nice layer of complexity. At Chicago, the issue of internal configuration is complicated by the need to

manage the transition from the openness and autonomy of the great parks to the enclosed architectural character of the quadrangles. This requires the integration of the sinewy, flowing qualities of Olmstedean space with the more geometrical layout of the quads to produce a kind of hybrid in which green spaces pour through an ordered complex of buildings. It also demands a series of seams between park and university, mappings of public and institutional territories, and reciprocal reinforcement of the special character of each.

There is a fundamental difference between the linearity and motility of the street and the centrality and calm of the quad. The medium of Cobb's reconciliation of grid and park was the "gothic" quad. This created both a series of linked, land-scaped courts and an urban street wall at the outermost edges of the original four-block superquad, which itself creates the possibility for the selective excision of streets. These excisions both allow structures that exceed the size of a block—athletic fields, hospital complex, and so on—and also provide the material precondition for the defining spatial strategy of the campus: the multiplication of the quads.

The Quads in Becoming ▽

A Sketch from the ▷
Romanesque Proposal
A View from the Midway ▽

Any expansion of the university must come to grips with the *idea* of the quads, with their defining quality as space. This is the central formal task of a master plan, to figure a series of spaces that will in scale, proportion, and quality inform the architecture that ultimately describes them. The architectural proposal in Cobb's first plan was precise, but generic, the individuality of the buildings of less immediate consequence than the spaces they were to make. This is a slightly tautological proposition as architectural "space" can only be produced by building, a relationship of reciprocity.

Cobb's quads—with their consistent scale and limited range of architectural expression—both resolve these conflicting claims and exhibit strong internal variety, some shady, some sunny, some with a strong feeling of walled enclosure, others more open. Although none of these spaces is itself complex, they create, in aggregate, a labyrinth. This feeling of the labyrinthine, of complication, of choices about how to exit, enter, cross, or circumnavigate a space, about alternatives, is critical to the spirit of the campus.

The Chicago scheme of revivalist architecture in an artificial landscape requires a third element: the simulacrum, the idea of the grafted expressive authority of defunct architectural style, as if Chicago really were Oxford, the view immortalized in those Thomas Hardy shots of the university rising over Washington Park (never Woodlawn). Although the choice of the collegiate gothic now seems naturalized both by association and longevity, the initial expressive choice was less clear-cut. Cobb himself first proposed a Romanesque revival image but was dissuaded by a pair of trustees who encouraged him to redo his plans in "the very latest English Gothic." For these advocates, the gothic bespoke both permanence and seriousness, a lofty, non-secular architecture, a ready-made for the ages.

Other possibilities were also abroad, however. The university opened at the same time and adjacent to the World's Columbian Exposition, the architectural highwater mark of the City Beautiful movement, the built, if temporary, exemplar of its planning philosophy. Extravagantly symmetrical and clad in sunny, neo-classical white, the fair was the confident model of urbanism of a republic secure and imperial, the architectural analogue to the Great White Fleet. An assembly of discrete monuments, it offered an outward looking architecture through which flowing, kinetic spaces—including a wonderful web of canals—passed, bearing their traffic to the distant corners of the American imperium. The fair had a tremendous impact, one of the most focused, consistent, and influential events in American architectural history.

The Exposition was renowned, however, both for its grand exhibition halls and broad canals and for its Midway, a space that continues to perplex university planners. The Midway was the social and architectural relief valve for the fair, where dubious entertainments and extravagant nonconforming architecture were located in eclectic profusion. To one side of this spectacle (visible in some period photographs) lay the early buildings of the university with their "Gothic" architecture, falling in with the Bavarian castles and Arabesque minarets of the Midway.

Across the Midway, however, lay yet another of the great monuments of the Fair: Frank Lloyd Wright's Midway Gardens, the architectural other that, from its Robie House outpost, haunts the campus to this day, the ghost of what might have been. Wright's beer garden, along with Sullivan's Transportation Building on the fair grounds, signaled that something even more radical than the fair was afoot.

This was the moment at which Chicago was in the process of reinventing architecture for the world, playing midwife to modernism. Like the fair, the university was born in repudiation of the contemporary, preferring, like so many other American campuses, historical drag, resuscitating a sputtering early nineteenth century revival rather than risking a role in the development of the new.

Robie House ▷

Despite this absence of innovation, however, the University of Chicago quickly grew into one of the world's finest academic ensembles, a set of spaces of great gravity and calm, built with craft and consistency and energized by the subtlety and proportion of the originating plan. The main quads, with their rich and solemn architecture, are beautifully proportioned and sequenced and the passage from one outdoor room to another perfectly captures the collegiate fantasy of the university's founders: one of the definitive signifiers of academe. Tremendously coherent and legibly singular, the quadrangles incorporate an articulate system of architectural variety that makes the whole rich rather than uniform.

This coherence is the product of a number of choices made early in the life of the university. The gothic revival architecture, by a number of architects, is extremely good and the proportions and relations of the aggregated spaces are superb. The scale of the original architecture—walkable by foot in both horizontal and vertical axes—keeps institutional divisions both unaggressive and effectively clear. Most of the early campus buildings are only a little larger than the domestic—academic mansions consonant with the surrounding residential scale. Furthermore, the decision to build consistently in limestone has had a strong and unifying effect, obscuring the more egregious architecture that has befallen the quads over the years.

This gothic campus developed rapidly and cohesively up to the Second World War. Like most institutions, however, the university gave up historicist building in the immediate postwar years. Policies since, with very mixed results, have

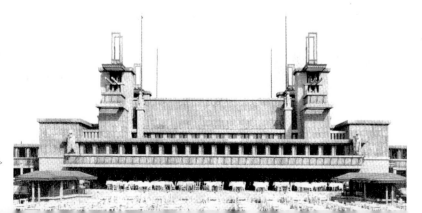

Midway Gardens ▷

Princeton △
West Point ▽

Yale △
Bryn Mawr ▽

Trinity College △
Harvard ▽

Duke △
Chicago ▽

continued to foreground the "idea" of the gothic while at the same time embracing the expressive palette of modernity, a strategy that has produced its share of freaks. Having abandoned literalism, however, the campus default in re-evoking the "gothic" has been impoverished, devolving into little more than limestone cladding and vague quadrangularity, if, on occasion, the university's architects have attempted more formal riffs via variations of scale, proportion, and detail.

Today, the compact that allowed Cobb's plan to proceed so successfully no longer holds. It isn't simply a question of the fading of the gothic, a style rich and codified enough to have allowed a variety of practitioners to work within its conventions. It's a question, rather, of a culture that has moved on from what is by now the revival of a revival of a revival; of a university engaged with building projects of a dramatically different scale than those imagined by Cobb; of a neighborhood context that has shifted decidedly; and of a sense of formal and social ecology that demands a more complex and nuanced view of planning. The university's approach—a version of the zoning practices more generally used in urban planning—seeks to codify coherence at the lowest common denominator, insisting on limestone and "quads" but inattentive to the declining relevance of this approach both culturally and in its ability to achieve results that resemble Cobb's original.

Lately, under the implicit sanction of postmodern practice, the university has undertaken a limited revival of its earlier revivalism. The Lab School and the Oriental Institute have completed small additions which mimic their original architecture. The Knapp Biology Building, the Center for Advanced Medicine, and the homely new Press Building are more ambiguous in their indebtedness but are checkered with clear semiotic cues to their dispersed historicity. In limited contexts, this is harmless enough. In larger doses it's a formula for mediocrity. It isn't simply a matter of trying to clone an architecture on the losing end of natural selection but of the very impossibility of constructing anything more than a trivial example. As carving and intricacy become less and less available on both the creative and the crafts ends and as budget requirements assure that the rich texture of leaded windows and wood paneling is transformed to snap-in mullions and sheet rock ornament, a dumbed-down, banal architecture emerges, an insult to the idea of context.

The Quads Today ▷
The University, 1931 ▽

Unfortunately, what began as a means for managing the threat of disparity is now the means for creating it. While the logic of maintaining a uniform materiality for campus building continues to be fairly compelling, this is hardly the whole story and has been repeatedly breached. The real problem is a style of abstraction that purges meaning but substitutes nothing new. The Ad Building is the poster child for this devolutionary "stripped" approach. Horizontally expressed and primitively massed with limestone walls and a little pitched roof, it recalls Marissa Tomei's line to Joe Pesci: "Like *you* blend..."

The boldest attempt at the gothic/modern hybrid is the deeply ironical Regenstein Library, designed by Walter Netsch, the most eccentric of the Chicago Skidmore, Owings, and Merrill partners. An obviously anguished work, the Reg is clad in limestone panels carved to resemble the striated concrete of contemporary "brutalist" architecture. Responding to overwhelming storage requirements, Netsch produced a huge building in which the gothicizing comes from the repetitive surface articulation of the great bulk of the building, quirkless. The Reg's a prison-house of knowledge, its architecture a throwback to the military gothic, not to the light-filled English perpendicular.

High Gothic architecture is full of glass and delicacy: the problem of the cathedral is height plus light. The Regenstein is best where it's thinnest, most transparent, and most highly articulated—especially the thin eastern wing of the building, as it rounds the corner to the front, obscuring its length. But the huge building relies too much on mechanical repetition, is too lacking in eccentricity,

Hutch ▷
The Reg ▽

and too orthogonal by half. And, unlike the uplifting vaults of Harper Library or Hutchinson Commons, the spaces within are incredibly mean, compressed under waffle slabs and furnished on the cheap with swastika-shaped carrels. High Gothic aspires to the skeletal and the vertical, not the compressive horizontality of the slab.

The Regenstein is also an enormous building. Much of the university's projected construction—the Interdivisional Research Building, the gym, the new business school, the expansion of the hospitals—is likewise mega-scaled. This on-going scale creep produces buildings many times the size of the structures originally envisaged by Cobb. There is a moment in this cycle of growth when one paradigm simply drifts into another. At the hospital complex, the "medieval" collegiate pattern runs up against its limits, becoming more urban as big sequenced open spaces lined by thin buildings are compressed to the scale of streets and yards, turning the quads inside out, reducing their interior spaces to service courts. Simply enlarging the quads does not cut it. The architecture is critical.

The quadrangles, however, have their own style of creating large volumes. Both the main quadrangles and the hospitals are mega-structures, huge interconnected architectures comprised of individual building increments, constructed over time. These mega-structures are formed by horizontal laminations of building, by a series of lateral connections that newer university construction—the Science Quadrangle or the South Campus most schematically—cannot bring itself to

The Reg ▷
Harper ▽

emulate. Indeed, the incrementally extendable, interconnected, laminar quad is brilliantly flexible and intrinsic to Cobb's originating concept. And, after all, what is the real efficiency of a single 400,000-square-foot laboratory building that only awaits subdivision among researchers?

While the idea of adding directly to such mega-scaled structures as Regenstein or the Field House would seem simply to compound the scale-creep problem, using them in reversing the tendency to treat every new building discretely is critical. This revived style of addition and incorporation should include both lateral connections—extensions of the labyrinth—and vertical layerings. With large and undistinguished buildings in particular, poor but sturdy architectural investments can be redeemed through adaptive reuse and tectonic transformation, through both formal and functional enrichment.

Managing such transformations requires a plan that does not merely assign locations to buildings but configures the spaces between them which, in turn, help configure the forms of the new buildings themselves. Each of those buildings, imagined additively, must contribute to the greater task of making space. A plan can stimulate creative solutions to those elements which it does not fully describe by focusing on the comprehensive design of the figural, flowing space of circulation and landscape that is so central to campus character: landscape becomes the medium of the plan. The plan must manage scale, extend the labyrinth of both external and internal circulation, attend to the figure of what is too often seen as ground, and add layers of texture and complexity to the existing condition.

The Preferred View of the Neighborhood △
Gown ▷

GOWN AND TOWN

Like monasteries, universities are intentional communities, the closest we come to quotidian utopia. Nowhere else do we build societies of such common purpose or so secure in their goals, their organization, their styles of hierarchy and governance. This academic experiment in creating place has a long history in the United States, building inventively on European models of both social and physical organization and producing what is, in many ways, America's most successful urbanism.

The university campus is an ideal form of the city and campus planning a privileged form of urban planning. Like a city, a campus supports a "complete" ecology, including an idea about community, an enclosed economy, urban density, clear physical boundaries, and a set of daily habits that are characteristic of town life. Indeed, the campus solves many of the problems that vex the city in general, including questions of movement and transportation, the relation of domestic life to the workplace, the management of an atmosphere of conviviality and engagement, the practices of environmental sustainability, the integration of old and new architectures, the introduction of technical innovation, the balance between the physical and the the virtual, and the architectural practices necessary to create urban identity.

Both city planning and campus planning put unusual faith in the physical: their logic is predicated on propinquity. Like the university itself, a campus plan promotes synergy, the intellectual and social benefit of having many people pursuing many disciplines in close assembly. As working adjacency is increasingly established by virtual means and immaterial networks, the campus continues to stand for the necessity and benefit of face to face contact. This is not simply a matter of engendering specific incidents of intellectual cross-fertilization but of creating a "community of scholars," of building an environment conducive to the free exchange of ideas.

When Cobb imagined the university, he had no anxiety about producing a master plan, a comprehensive vision of a physical environment, imagined down to its details. This "all-at-once" approach proposes a more contingent relationship between architecture and place. Today, however, we have become anxious about such unhesitatingly prescriptive styles of planning, about a style of projective homeostasis that seems to rule out chance.

It should surprise no one that such planning is greeted with deep suspicion. The experience of modernist planning with its own totalizing version of the all-at-once—which reached its nadir in projects like the Robert Taylor Homes, architecture as pure repression, served on a platter of "it's good for you"—has left both planners and citizens running scared. To many, the idea of the master plan seems irretrievably tied to the sinister history of "mastery," to centralization and authoritarianism. No need to recount the story of the university's role in Hyde Park's urban renewal save to say that it forms both the basis of community anxiety about the university's plans and establishes much of the structure of the neighborhood of today: neat modernist row houses and streets denuded of commerce to the north, devastation to the south. As a lifeless 55th Street bears witness, the university killed its own environment in an effort to save it.

Today's alpha model for both campus and urban growth is developmental and local, an inductive style of decision-making that contrasts with the top-down mode of climax urbanism. Such a starting-small strategy has as its virtue the possibility of fashioning strong contextual reactions, of improvisation, of flexibility. Like the city in general, such styles also embody a fantasy of free democratic decisions within a loose order. This preference for induction rises from contemporary revaluing not simply of the local but of the historic. If any approach characterizes contemporary American planning, it is the preservationist in both the architectural and social senses, an outgrowth, in part, of discontent with the ravages of plans too large and too blind.

The university's current planning strategy is loaded in favor of such an approach. Broad consultation with various campus constituencies has yielded a series of insights into specific spatial needs and locational possibilities. Buildings are assigned to available sites, architects hired to execute them, and the all-at-once emerges at the end of the process. There's no reimagination of the idea of site, no malleability to the big picture. The conceit that enables this is that the university already possesses a planning default, the quadrangle, sufficiently strong and clear conceptually and practically to allow, as with the Cobb plan, a policy of insertion, rather than a rigorous rethinking of the whole.

However, though modernist planning ideology surely deserved what it got and more inductive styles of planning are critical practices for enfranchisement and local sensitivity, something has nevertheless been lost. Not every all-at-once oppresses, particularly if it symbolizes values that are shared. Indeed, the all-at-once is a crucial mode of inquiry into exactly what those values are. Moreover, the anticipated scale of university construction, the energy and investment it implies, will have strong effects beyond the immediate collection of sites. A big plan is required by the interdependence of campus and neighborhood ecologies, by the university's obligations of community service and cooperation, and by the foundering formal sense of the campus all-at-once.

At a university symposium about community relations in 1999, a community activist claimed to see any public improvements to infrastructure in poor neighborhoods as a threat, the harbinger of gentrification. Community fear and the university's own beloved myths of beleaguerment conspire to frustrate the aspirations of both. Like the United States after Vietnam, the university suffers from post-urban renewal syndrome and an anxiety about the appearance of encroachment.

The plan presented here assumes that the future of the university is tied directly to the future of its surroundings, both formally and socially. It also asserts that the planning principles embodied in the historic campus—values of pedestrianism, landscape integration, mixed use, tractable scale, architectural quality, and community access—are important and good values that the university should be proud to extend and to share. As an architectural proposition, this plan frankly elides town and gown in the belief that there are urban principles that both can

55th Street, 1948 ▽

55th Street, 1999 ▽

happily share to their mutual betterment. The master plan, with its potential for transparency, energy, cooperation, and hope, can be an important means of bridging the gap between town and gown.

The university enjoys rare advantages in its surroundings. Public green and recreational spaces are abundant. The neighborhoods to the north and east are well-textured and substantial, mixing a useful variety of residential types. The bubbling local economy—should it continue to bubble—will rapidly fill these neighborhoods out and will, if successfully managed, have an impact to the south and, ultimately, to the west as well, where stable and culturally rich African-American neighborhoods could profoundly enlarge the university's own environment.

A plan is the concretization of desire. Its excitement lies both in its components and in a vision of their interaction. The fallacy of current planning is that this vision can simply be induced, that, as an artistic project, it's reasonable to take a chance on the prospective all-at-once based on the competence of its components. But, without an artistry that is specific to the whole, the university risks producing less than the sum of its parts.

EXISTING

 PROPOSED

A Masterplan for the University of Chicago ▽

55TH STREET COMMERCIAL CORRIDOR

COLLEGIATE VILLAGE
UNDERGROUND PARKING   ARTS COMPLEX

NORTH CAMPUS
IDR BUILDING   NATATORIUM

COLLEGIATE VILLAGES   OMNIPAIDEUM
NEW SCIENCE QUAD

COLLEGIATE VILLAGE

DINOSAUR MUSEUM   COLLEGIATE VILL
WEST CAMPUS   OLD CAMPUS

HOSPITAL GROWTH   COLLEG

SPORTS
FIELDS   MED SCHOOL QUAD

MIDWAY CHANNEL

60TH STREET BOULEVARD
COLLEGIATE VILLAGE

COMMUNITY QUAD   SOCIAL SERVICE QUAD
SOUTH CAMPUS   LAW QUAD

61ST ST

WOODLAWN GARDENS

63RD STREET COMMERCIAL CORRIDOR

A Master Plan for the University of Chicago ▽

57TH STREET COMMERCIAL CORRIDOR

AGE

MIDWAY BRIDGES

PARKING

USINESS QUAD

MERCIAL CORRIDOR

◁ *North Campus*
Massing Study

NORTH CAMPUS

Because to build-all-at-once was infeasible, a number of vital elements were left out of the first wave of university construction, including a library and a gymnasium. As a stopgap, the university built—on the site currently occupied by Harper Court—a temporary brick building to house the library, the gym, and the university press, including its printing plant. Although born of convenience, the mixture is intriguing: one contemplates students sweaty and energized from working out passing directly into the hush of the stacks. *Mens sana in corpore sano*!

Any development of the north campus will similarly involve such polyfurcations and should energetically manage the mix. The variety of uses presently on site— library, athletics, residences, museum, administration, offices, classrooms, etc.— should be retained and enlarged upon even as physical coherence and connections to the satisfying textures and propositions of the main quads are deepened. Like that early mixed-use building, this richly cross-programmed environment has tremendous potential to develop a unique and stimulating sense of place.

Architecturally, the situation is somewhat confused. Although the north campus— from 55th to 57th Streets and from Ellis to University Avenues—is exactly the same size as the main quadrangles, the existing quads are a masterpiece of both complexity and coherence, almost seamlessly built according to a consistent set of architectural conventions. The area to the north lacks spatial coherence, designed according to a shifting set of planning values, a Pirandelloesque collection of isolated structures in search of an architectural reason to coexist.

Mixed Use ▷

The north campus is also characterized by extreme disparities in scale. Ranging from the smallish Smart Museum to the high-rise Pierce Tower, to the very large Field House, to the huge Regenstein Library, the north campus simply will not support a solution based entirely on the thin peripheral buildings and orthogonal quadscape of the original campus. Creating "super-quads" by adding buildings around the periphery of the blocks will never duplicate the intimate, smaller-scaled character of the existing quads, however compelling the arguments may be from the perspective of the streetscape. Indeed, if any location on campus needs a singular, comprehensive vision, this is it. Turning it into a dumping ground for orphaned uses is not good enough: just as a parking structure on the main quads is an unimaginable sacrilege, placing one on the north campus guarantees that it will never attain the serenity of the original.

The Gordian Knot of the north campus is the Regenstein Library. The Reg is the anti-quad, a huge mass dumped in the middle of the block, a Baroque axis-terminator of the first water, and the death of the interior figuration of its block. The Reg, in its enormity and opacity, has a powerful aura, manipulating the reading of scale of any building within its ambit. And it's a circulation killer: the Reg destroys the possibility of directly extending the main north-south axis of the campus. By closing off this flow, the Regenstein imposes a tremendous obstacle to everything to its north, walling it off from the center of gravity of the main quads, forcing motion to detour around it.

North Campus Study ◁
Cut the Gordian Knot! ▷

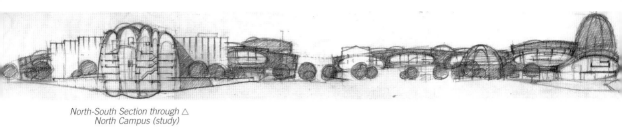

North-South Section through △
North Campus (study)

North Campus Master Plan ▽

The best solution is to open it up. At a minimum, this entails an entrance from the north. But why not consider more radical surgery that opens the north-south route, expands the library, ameliorates its grim interior, lays in a learning infrastructure for the 21st century, and creates a new center for campus life? Why not the creation of an Omnipaideum, a place for gathering and disseminating information in all media, a hive of storage and exchange? While reverencing the book is central to the civil religion of the university, the new millennium demands the elevation of other technologies of record. The university might leapfrog the competition in the creation of a very new kind of site for learning.

One of my happiest undergraduate memories is of studying in the reading rooms in Harper Library. That remarkable sequence of spaces was the internal version of the connected spaces of the quads. The rooms were remarkably diverse, ranging from vaulted Law to heroic Harper, to low Social Science, to gemlike Classics, (with the poetry room up in the tower). These were rooms of enormous dignity. With their long, heavy, oak tables and elaborate detail, the range of physical differences they supported and the pattern of circulation they set up, they also produced a remarkable social environment. Elaborate rituals of status and affinity went into choosing where to study (Classics was for the coolest, its denizens reading the Phaedrus in Greek, smoking Gitanes in the corridor). This aestheticization of the space of scholarship and the ceremonies of learning is a crucial way in which the university supports the importance of its mission.

Imagine the Regenstein Omnipaideum. From its glazed central gallery and vertical circulation court, a sequence of study spaces would radiate in various scales and registers: open, secluded, collective, alone. A link to Bartlett would capture the lofty upstairs gym for a reading room, and study balconies could project into the central gallery from adjacent reading areas. A large new study space—focused on electronic media—could be grafted to the west edge of the building, linked by a strong cross-axial route to the center. Like the village life that clustered around the walls and bulk of medieval fortified towns, small-scaled uses could proliferate at the perimeter of Regenstein's mass and along a new

NATATORIUM APPLICANT POOL OMNIPAEDEUM LIBRARY EXPANSION & ACADEMIC SPACE COLLEGE HOUSING

internal distributor that included both gym space and the buildings of the science quads. These new spaces might include classrooms and lecture theaters, small exhibition and performance spaces, start-up space for new departments and committees—an incubator for cross-fertilization and innovation as well a complex interior circulation spine to foster intercommunication. And, of course, those indispensible cafes would dot this landscape, break-out spaces for social life and heated discussions.

Opening Regenstein along the north-south axis would also dramatically clarify the relationship of the existing quadrangles to the north campus. Such a cut (a forgotten recommendation of the 1998 Kristner study) not only acknowledges the north-south energy of the main quad, creating a richer, more "gothic" environment, but it could also exploit interesting possibilities for physical and functional connectedness, rather than continuing the current regime of structures too much imagined in isolation. Especially at a moment when the university is thinking about projects—labs, parking, gym, etc.—that have extremely large footprints, special care must be taken to preserve the sense of labyrinth that is so crucial to a reading of "gothic" planning and to securing the sequence of greenspaces that, in their seriality and proportion, define a sense of the quads. The simultaneous elaboration of Regenstein and the remainder of the north

Looking South Over 56th Street ◁
North Campus Massing Studies ▽

Looking North Over 57th Street △

Looking West △

55th and Ellis △

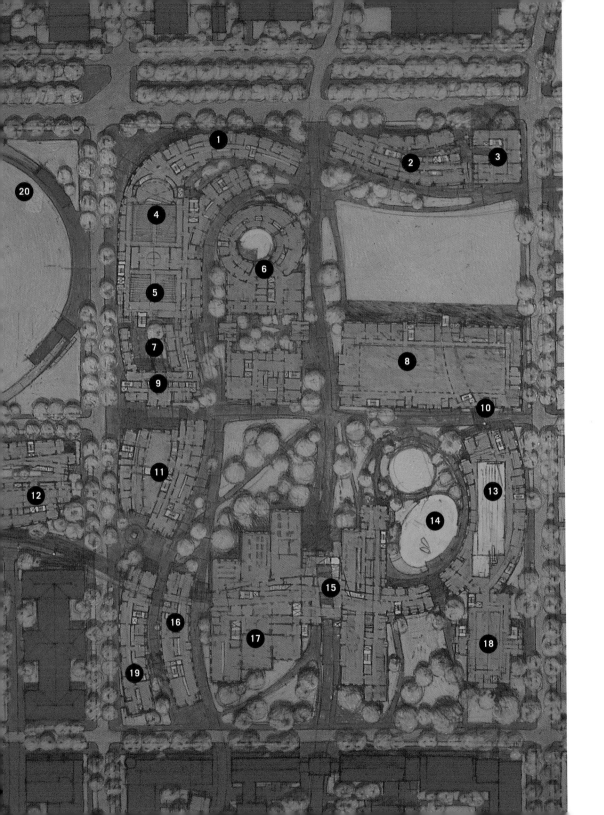

campus offers an opportunity to produce a new site of interactive density and, in its remarkable mix of uses, a new kind of environment, filled with complex interactions among users, uses, and buildings. Like the gothic quads, in which a series of connected buildings produce a mega-structure that usefully blurs the relationship of individual buildings to each other and to the whole, the organization of the north campus stands metaphorically for the larger mission of the university. The literal connectedness of structures not simply raises the stakes architecturally, but obliges a synergy in which the sense of place on campus is always conceived as greater than the sum of its parts.

North Campus Study, Plan at Grade ◁

This kind of joinery, however, does not simply serve to create linkages, it establishes enclosure. The identity of individual quads and campus spaces arises from their legibility as figures, from the texture of their landscapes, and from the quality of their architectural boundaries. This is a reciprocating relation in which both the space of the quads and the mass of its envelope create much of each other's character. Buildings too tall, too large, too thick, or too singular can overpower a space. Conversely, a strong space can go a long way toward uniting architectural disparity.

The Science Quadrangle offers a useful cautionary tale. Disconnected, dissimilarly designed, and architecturally undistinguished buildings fail to cohere despite a

1	CAFE, COMMERCIAL SPACE, LOFTS & HOUSING ABOVE	11	COLLEGE HOUSING
2	COMMONS / COLLEGE HOUSING ABOVE	12	INTERDIVISIONAL RESEARCH BUILDING
3	PIERCE TOWER REMADE	13	NATATORIUM
4	1500-SEAT THEATER	14	APPLICANT POOL
5	NEW COURT THEATER	15	REGENSTEIN CROSSING
6	SMART GROWTH	16	OMNIPAIDEUM GROWTH
7	ARTISTS IN RESIDENCE STUDIOS	17	OMNIPAIDEUM
8	RECONFIGURED FIELD HOUSE	18	BARTLETT
9	ART HISTORY	19	HOUSING/ ACADEMIC
10	BRIDGE OF THIGHS	20	UNDERGROUND PARKING

preponderance of limestone. Proportions are unrelated, there are too many strategies for creating windows and other openings, and no sense of harmony in managing transparency and opacity. Dominating the space, the savagely ugly Crerar library—a parti simply lifted off the shelf—is designed with clumsy inapt horizontality. Space leaks from the quad, the landscaping is vapid, and the two-level, bermed arrangement makes no sense. And all of the buildings on the quad, with the exception of the library, have their priority, their front doors, on the street, their backs (never mind a door) to the quad. The Science Quad needs a reformulation of circulation to favor access from the interior, the plugging of a couple of gaps in the space with small scale construction, and re-landscaping.

The north campus is something else. Larger in scale, it has the potential to become a distinct university neighborhood. And, like any neighborhood, it should be thought of in terms of self-sufficiency and a sense of completion, its own all-at-once. This requires a critical mass of residents on the site, a population at work, attention to athletics, recreation, and body-culture, as well as a raft of neighborhood amenities. Located in a corner of Hyde Park that is virtually unserved commercially, the north campus has the potential to become both a campus and a community center. Imagine a grocery store, a cafe, a good Italian restaurant, a laundromat, a news dealer...

Lying in effect on a middle ground between the quads and the existing neighborhood, the north campus should draw characteristics from both and should strongly enhance its relationship to 55th Street and to Ellis. Underconceptualized 55th Street retains the potential to become a boulevard, lined with buildings and commerce, joining the Chicago parkway system in an elegant sequence from Midway Airport to the lake. This more urban sense of density might also turn the corner, and head down a reinforced Ellis, the logical site for sidewalk cafes and a theatrical complex enlarging the Court Theater. These and other new and existing uses—athletics, galleries, Omnipaedum, housing, labs, offices, lofts, classrooms, shops, etc.—would guarantee high levels of traffic around the clock, supplementing the more singular style of use on the main quads.

North Campus Study, Roof Plan ▷

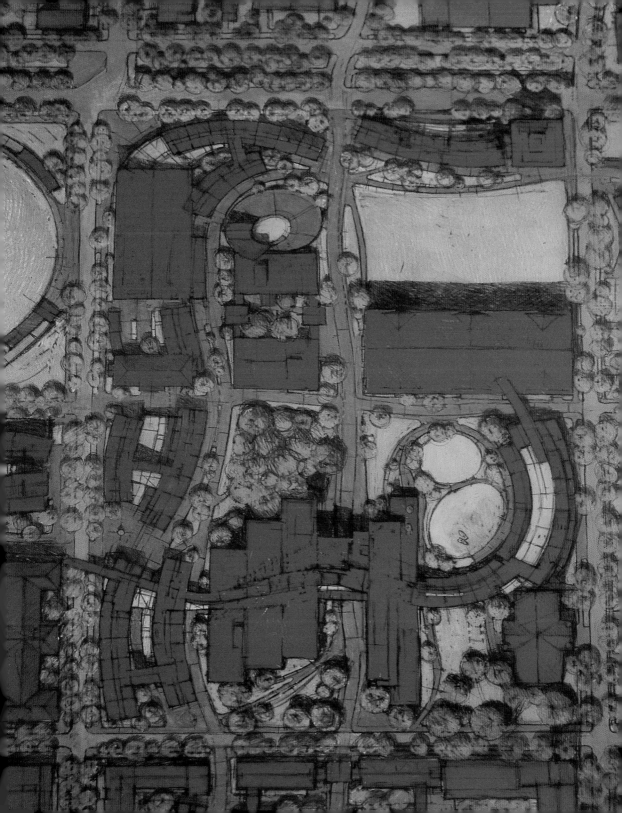

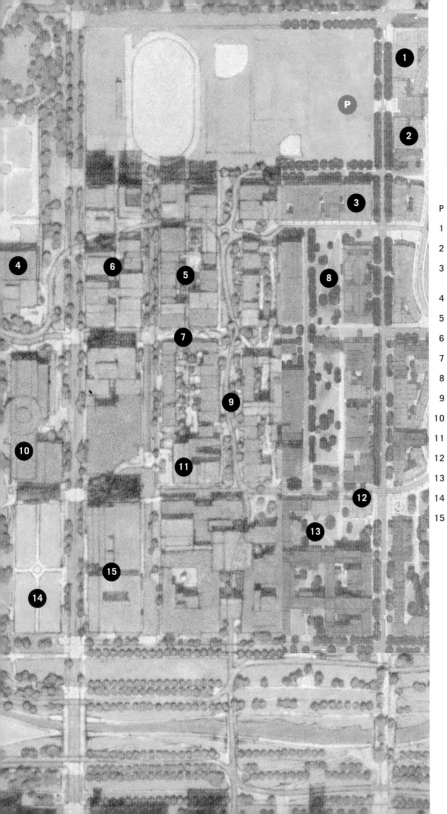

EXISTING

PROPOSED

P PARKING UNDER STAGG FIELD

1 LARGE THEATER

2 ARTS COMPLEX

3 INTERDIVISIONAL
RESEARCH BUILDING

4 DuSABLE MUSEUM

5 COLLEGIATE VILLAGES

6 HOUSING / ACADEMIC / HOSPITAL

7 COMMERCIAL STRIP

8 NEW SCIENCE QUAD

9 GREENWAY

10 DINOSAUR MUSEUM

11 HOSPITAL EXPANSION

12 NEW AD

13 MED SCHOOL QUAD

14 GARDENS OR SPORTS FIELDS

15 HOSPITAL EXPANSION

WEST SIDE

Planning an unfolding succession of quadlike figural spaces and a logical set of links between variegated activities on the north campus is greatly aided by the existence of several ready-mades, including 55th Street, the broad expanse of the athletic fields, and Washington Park. These large and dramatic elements of spatial infrastructure beg a special architectural response. Like the edge of the Midway or, more grandly, like the buildings around Central Park in Manhattan, these edges should be attractors for architecture that takes special advantage of the light, view, and sense of boundary they describe.

These great spaces are the key armature for the campus west of Ellis, itself another logical all-at-once. An elegant line of buildings along the south side of 56th Street, beginning as labs and new commons space (the Accelerator Building has potential for conversion), continuing as residences and then turning the corner to join the range of hospital buildings, would be a logical strategy for growth—an L-shaped, big-scaled enclosure, a hyper-quad. At the park corner, the size of the buildings could be increased, beginning to scale up all four edges of Washington Park. At present, the park adds little value to its surroundings architecturally or socially. While holding numerous recreational and cultural sites and opportunities, the park also has, like a beautiful quandrangle at the urban scale, the possibility of entering into a far stronger and more productive relationship with its perimeter.

Growth of the hospitals is likely to continue its movement north along Cottage Grove. This is an opportunity both to describe a beautiful campus edge and to concentrate uses—patient care, residences, offices—that take advantage of the view of greenery and sunsets over the park lagoon. At present, what is arguably the finest site on the west campus, the northwest corner of the Midway, is occupied by a parking structure. This is a terrible waste and calls for a major piece of architecture. Washington Park, like the Midway, is the university's front yard and both park and campus stand to benefit from greater mutual interaction.

1	DINOSAUR MUSEUM	7	SMART MUSEUM
2	DuSABLE MUSEUM	8	MANDEL HALL
3	RENAISSANCE SOCIETY	9	ORIENTAL INSTITUTE
4	REGENSTEIN COLLECTIONS	10	HYDE PARK HISTORICAL SOCIETY
5	COURT THEATER	11	MUSEUM OF SCIENCE AND INDUSTRY
6	NEW THEATER	12	HYDE PARK ART CENTER

P MAJOR PARKING

COMMERCIAL STRIP

Of related interest to university growth is the complex of buildings, already in the park. The DuSable Museum, in particular, forms a western anchor to a remarkable string of cultural institutions, including the Smart Museum, the Renaissance Society, the Regenstein Gallery, the Oriental Institute, and the Museum of Science and Industry. The potential for synergies among these institutions is enormous and might be augmented by the conversion of the beautiful circular building belonging to the Parks District—what better spot for Paul Serrano's dinosaur museum—and by the support of other small public and commercial galleries. Potential locations for these include the expanded Omnipaideum, new commercial spaces on the north campus stretch of 55th Street, and a number of locations along 57th Street, the logical main axis of this cultural corridor.

Within the west campus, the situation is more delicate. In the block to the west of Ellis, there's a clear opportunity to create either a linear chain of small quadrangles or, more boldly, a single mall-like space, a mini-Midway. These spaces would create a flow from the Midway to the athletic fields, perhaps to include a new Stagg Field with proper bleachers (easily combined with a complex of squash courts or other athletic uses) for athletic competition and other large-scale campus events. This sequence of spaces might be enlarged by the redesign of the corner of 58th and Ellis to make a more graceful westward transition from the main quads. The suggestion presented here entails the demolition of the Ad Building and the relocation of its functions to the other side of Ellis, looking back to the campus; the construction of a dining and student center and plaza kitty-cornered from it (on part of the old Ad site); the creation of a large plaza on Ellis adjacent to the new Ad Building; the relocation of surgical suites to a more convenient location; and the creation of a new building quadrangle, and more formal entrance and identity for the Medical School.

More locally, the concatenation of arts and cultural institutions in Hyde Park stands to realize great mutual benefits through a clarification of their own spatial relations. The development of the 57th Street corridor from park to park could have a substantial impact on the university's atmosphere and on the perception of it as a place apart. These cultural institutions, directed at the public, are vital to the kind of mood and purpose that represent the university at its best.

THE SOUTH BANK

In the space of a single block the university neighborhood goes from affluence to rubble. Perhaps a new name (SoMi?, SoBa?) would begin to restore some sense of mutuality and hope. More urgent is a planning strategy that includes the Midway, the South Campus, Woodlawn, and the 63rd Street corridor. Ironically, the current Dresdenlike state of many of the blocks south of 61st Street offers an opportunity for progressive transformation and, with it, the overthrow of the apartheid that has too long characterized the university's relations with its neighbors to the south. Reinforced by a *cordon sanitaire* of parking lots and hurricane fencing—the south campus has too long been a barrier across which nothing is meant to be diffused.

The Midway is the Maginot Line, dividing the campus, a huge linear space with two very long edges. Conceptually, the Midway was planned as a connector between two large green spaces. Functionally, it's a boulevard, parking lot, and informal university play space. Visually, it's a muddy, under-designed, inaccessible mall that organizes nothing. And finally, there's that remnant aura, the raffish whiff of Little Egypt and other non-intellectual entertainments. Denuded of the stately elms that once lined it, ragged and unkempt, its best served users are cars. What to do with it?

Although arguments of original intent can be thorny, Olmsted's initial notion that the Midway be a waterway, a link in a chain of lagoons flowing from Lake Michigan to Washington Park, is a wonderful one. Ironically, aquifying the Midway, making it into more of a physical boundary, might make it far easier to cross. By adding a promenade-lined channel, traversed by a succession of beautiful bridges, aswim with punts and shells and water taxis (the Gleacher Center, and step on it!), and filled with skaters in winter, crossing the Midway might become delightful. This would require a major municipal address to traffic (this plan suggests boulevardizing 60th Street and removing the center lanes from the Midway) but the infrastructure-fixation of the current city administration brings this within reason.

MIDWAYS

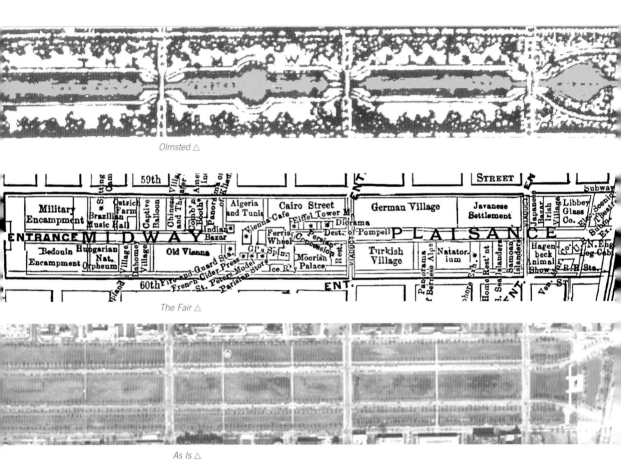

Olmsted △

The Fair △

As Is △

Architecturally, the response of university buildings to the Midway varies dramatically from side to side. On the north, the continuous mass of the hospitals and the quads provides a solid, well-scaled edge, a limestone mountain range. East of University Avenue, the paradigm shifts to a series of discrete architectural objects, the most prominent of which is Rockefeller Chapel. On the south side, this pattern is absolute: a series of detached, horizontally proportioned, monumental buildings, each isolated in its own plot—a small Washington Mall. This pattern is problematized by the fact the main address of these buildings, unlike the "two way" character of the buildings on the quads, is the Midway, setting up a strong hierarchy of front and back and creating the present DMZ of parking lots. Transforming this strip will entail both offering a dignified university face along 61st Street and creating two inward faces within the depth of the block.

To galvanize SoMi, the south campus needs to be rescued from its own incompleteness. It is logical that the South Bank become home to a string of worldly professional schools: SSA, Law, and Business. The relocation of the GSB is clearly the major issue. At present, the argument is a little circular. The GSB prefers not to move to a marginal part of campus but the only solution to this marginality is a commitment to move large resources to the vacant land south of the Midway. Indeed, the "problem" of the south campus lies in its lack of a critical mass of activities to animate it, in its lack of internal connections, and in its back turned to Woodlawn.

METRA

MIDWAY BRIDGES

P

1 COMMUNITY QUAD

2 SOCIAL SERVICE QUAD

3 COLLEGIATE VILLAGE

4 LAW QUAD

5 BUSINESS QUAD

6 61ST STREET RENEWED

7 METRA

P PARKING

Moving the GSB would turn this situation around dramatically. Sited at the east end of the Midway, the GSB would have enough space to configure its campus freely and to grow, and would provide an "anchor" for that corner of the campus. This site is ideal from the perspective of access, offering the possibility of a direct rail connection as well as an excellent location for a large parking structure. There are sufficient buildings on the site, including the Ed Stone dorm, a pretty good gothic revival office building, the new Press Building and the Orthogenic complex, to provide a context for new construction. The current revival of the south side of 61st Street calls out for an appropriately stimulating northern neighbor. The GSB might both offer this and sponsor low-key commercial development along its end of the street.

A new GSB would join the row of modern monuments along the south edge of the Midway. This is an interesting collection of buildings from a very particular, even poignant, moment of the mitosis of modernism into post, a museum of the re-birth of representationalism. Mies van der Rohe's SSA is the classic statement of modernist orthodoxy: black glass and steel, the building concedes nothing, a temple on the park. Saarinen's elegant Law Building folds its Miesian glass curtain wall in abstract emulation of the complexities of the gothic and sits behind a forecourt, open to the Midway, too unenclosed to be called a quad but clearly feinting at it. Edward Durrell Stone's former Center for Continuing Education is a vaguely Islamicized classical temple, utterly Sixties in its confidence, red carpets, and hermetic affect. The dopey Press Building simply returns to the brain-dead mimesis that produced such gems as the Ad.

Existing △

"Infill" Scheme △

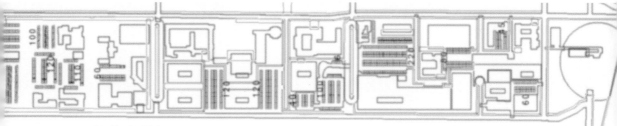

"Parking Lot" Scheme △

Woodlawn Dresden △
Building Sites ▽

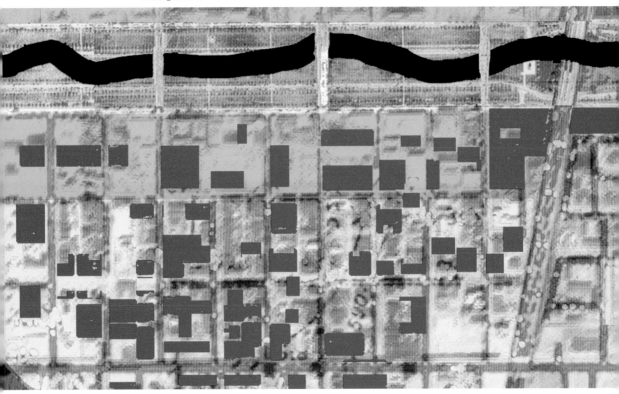

Woodlawn Revived ▽

This architectural melange offers, in both its style and its gaps, great latitude for the GSB to commission a major work that signals its own aspirations to comprehend and influence the radically transformed global economic environment at the millennium. The generous site permits the development of a real quadrangle, embracing academic, residential, athletic, and recreational spaces, and might include both a gym and a commons to be shared with its south campus neighbors. A bonus would be the potential availability of a portion of Burton-Judson for graduate housing.

The most delicate question, though, is the meeting of the campus and Woodlawn. A comprehensive plan has the virtue both of clarifying university intentions and of demonstrating its willingness to be both good neighbor and— as the local 500-pound gorilla—to undertake sympathetic improvements in the wider neighborhood. A beginning is to build the university side of 61st Street with appropriate scale and gravity, with clearly elaborated moments of entry, and with shared town/gown uses. These might include further elaboration of the present social service facilities (perhaps a center for community entrepreneurship run by the GSB), residential and commercial spaces, and, especially, green and recreational spaces.

These park and garden spaces would make a fine medium of transition, flowing from the new southern quadrangles into the community, forming a variety of squares, parks, and play areas to help re-establish character in those ravaged blocks. University assistance in the creation of a network of greenspaces for Woodlawn would contribute to a strong Chicago tradition of interpolated figural green spaces, as embodied so strikingly in sites like Madison Park. Finally, the university might help the redevelopment and greening of 63rd Street, critical as the nearest logical concentration of commercial activity for the south campus as well as the historic main street of Woodlawn.

63rd Street Revived ▷

1 MEDICAL CENTER

2 UNIVERSITY OF ILLINOIS

3 NATURAL HISTORY COMPLEX

4 CONVENTION CENTER

5 ILLINOIS INSTITUTE OF TECHNOLOGY

6 LINE OF THOUGHT

7 WATER TAXI TO EVANSTON & THE LOOP

8 TECHNOLOGY ZONE

9 MUSEUM OF SCIENCE AND INDUSTRY

10 UNIVERSITY OF CHICAGO

11 KING COLLEGE

SOUTH SIDE SYNERGY

To remain competitive with its larger, better-endowed peer institutions, the university requires a leap that can only be based on strategic alliances. The south side of Chicago is incredibly well equipped with the kind of cultural, institutional, and academic muscle that could make this possible. Within a few miles of the campus lie IIT, in the midst of self-revitalization, the expanding Circle Campus of the University of Illinois, the biomedical complex centered on County Hospital, the natural history compound grouped around the Field Museum, King College, and numerous secondary and other schools, not to mention the grouping of institutions around the university.

Here's the fantasy: what if these institutions vigorously pursued a series of formal and informal links to share academic and development resources. And, what if this chain of institutions were to be physically linked by a "line of thought," a trolley system running north-south on a very frequent schedule. Finally, to spin this out a little more, what if these institutions were to sponsor a development together?

As the demolition of the Taylor Homes proceeds, something far better should take their place. Recognizing not simply the tremendous human and intellectual resources of the south side but also its potential tractability and the broad future direction of American productivity, it seems both compelling and logical that energy be focused on creating an economic and intellectual driver for the resurgence of the south side. That the location of this driver be well-linked, well-served, and legible can only be a plus.

The south side, now booming, holds vast unbuilt areas, including a potentially magnificent complex of sites along the Chicago River. Lacking, though, is an obvious location for the kinds of synergistic activity that have made the success of places like Kendall Square in Cambridge or the Stanford and Princeton research parks. As a preliminary suggestion, the territory from Garfield north, between State Street and the Expressway, could become an in-city hi-tech zone, an incubator and a focus for knowledge-based industry of the future.

COLLEGIATE VILLAGES

COMMONS

GRADUATE AND MIXED HOUSING

HOUSING THE COLLEGE

At present, Hyde Park and the university provide students with living possibilities that are, at best, eclectic. This is, in many ways, a strength—there are choices, including dorms, university apartments, and the private market. But the fact of choice is not enough: the question is also one of particulars. I remember my own experience in Pierce Tower. After a year in a concrete cubicle with a university-chosen roommate, I couldn't wait to move into a legendary Hyde Park apartment. There was a serious cachet attached to living "outside" the system, if only the dorm system.

The lack of a coherent physical structure for the College (and the university's decision to tear down a major dorm) represents a chance to start over from close to scratch. Although holding a reasonably large number of beds, the university's residential system lacks presence, certainly nothing to compare with Cambridge Colleges or Harvard Houses, the Latin Quarter, or Greenwich Village. But an interesting skeleton is there. The core of the dorm system is presently the 100-person "house," a logical increment for future development. We support both the idea that the basic unit of residential identity be the house and that those houses be relatively small and be deployed in various configurations. Obscuring the individuality of the houses, a la Pierce Tower, Woodward Court, the Shoreland, or the new dormitory, does not produce the maximum benefit that the small scale of the houses might enable.

This plan proposes augmenting the 100-person house with a smaller, 20- to 30-person type. These smaller houses would both function to encourage a different style of living and would allow greater utilization of existing building stock and the opportunity to knit small structures into a variety of residual locations around the campus. The small scale of these houses would add to communal identity, provide designers with a strong prejudice towards the kind of additive, incremental growth that characterizes the quads, help prevent major architectural mistakes, and produce smaller, more highly fundable units. It would also provide a greater sense of diversity, density, and complexity for the system and originate a physical field on which the university residence system could establish its own lexicon of arcana, aiding the emergence of a post-gothic vernacular.

1 DEWEY COLLEGE

2 INDEPENDENT HOUSES

3 GREY COLLEGE

4 HUTCHINS COLLEGE

5 CHANDRASEKHAR COLLEGE

6 REDFIELD COLLEGE

7 ARENDT COLLEGE

COMMONS

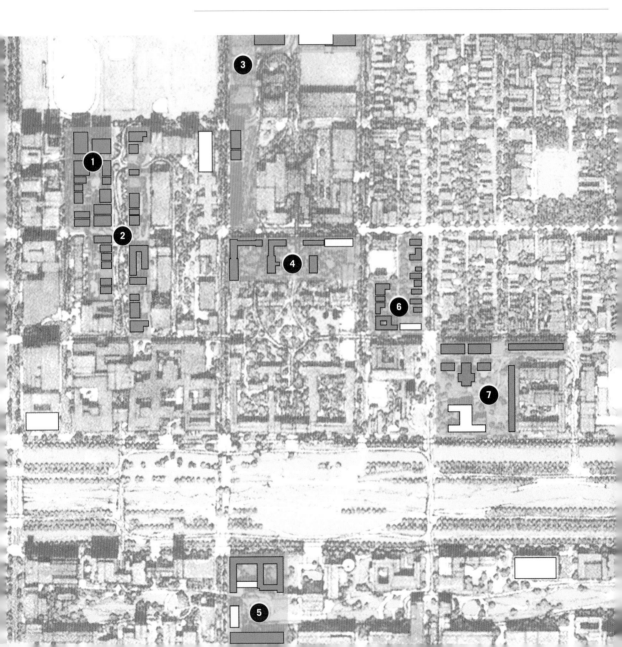

This possibility would be further enhanced by employing a range of architectural types, including high-rises, walk-ups, mews, and row housing, as well as small "residules" inserted in accommodating gaps on campus. A variety of internal arrangements—from individual dorm rooms to apartments to lofts—might be included rather than promoting a basically uniform type—the classic dorm *existenzminimum*—that characterizes present thinking. Such a complex set of interesting choices might come to be a visible singularity of the Chicago system, another reason to come to the College.

The current system of houses and commons could also be expanded to form the substrate of a series of larger campus communities. The word "village" (used by Ed Barnes in his north campus proposal of the Sixties) is a good one to describe a style of aggregation that embraces the legibility of its individual parts while still offering a cohesive feeling of something larger. Each of these new villages might include houses of various sizes; a commons for dining, student activities, and athletics; staff residences; academic space; and commercial space. Each village would develop its own distinctive physical and social character and with it a set of relationships and loyalties that are the bedrock of any community. An alumna might, for example, want to donate a new house to the village in which she lived during her college years.

We propose seven locations for these collegiate villages. The first replaces Woodward Court and incorporates Ida Noyes as its commons; the second converts the CTS building (should it become available), linking it via a glazed inner court with the university-owned houses on University and Woodlawn Avenues. The third would convert the group of small, ideally-sized, biological sciences buildings in the Hull group and utilize Hutch and possibly part of Bartlett as commons space. The fourth would be located along 55th Street and Ellis Avenue (including a renovated Pierce) and would have its commons in a transformed Pierce Commons. A fifth village might be situated in and around the block bounded by 56th, 57th, Drexel, and Maryland with potential expansion to the parkfront to the west. A sixth village would expand on Burton-Judson and a final site would aggregate a group of small houses along Drexel.

Such an eclectic yet dense arrangement would be unique in American higher education and might well become a signature of the Chicago system. And, by the intense utilization of existing, historic resources, the character of these villages would not have to be created *ex novo* but would enjoy instant texture and patina, allowing the university to house students in some of its most historic and beautiful structures. These villages could support an expanded idea of the academic commons, each of which would embrace a far wider range of activities—including classrooms, athletic facilities, offices, libraries, commercial facilities, and so on—than are currently supported. Such comprehensive local centers become especially vital in the context of a dramatically expanded college which risks the loss of intimacy and contact of a smaller one.

Universities are strong models of governance. All members of the university community have multiple affiliations within it, including house, commons, department, school, etc., most of which are freely chosen. The residential system is crucial to this structure of community, especially in the lives of undergraduates. However, if the system is to play a central role in the organization of student governance, something must be done to include those who opt not to live within the system. One possibility is to elevate the role of the commons to something beyond a service site, creating a bicameral affiliation house and commons. All students might thus become members of one of the commons for purposes of governance and other activities. Indeed, the choice of commons might be independent of the choice of house, encouraging a variety of cross-campus affiliations.

Of course, quality of student life is not simply the product of university facilities. Hyde Park hasn't enough of the sense of street-life that is a hallmark of urbanity. The university confronts a special challenge in both seeding its own sites with the kinds of uses—cafes, shops, lounges, sports facilities—that are indispensable to student life and in guiding the commercial revival of Hyde Park and Woodlawn in a way that encourages both services useful to the academic community and multiple sites for varied interaction between town and gown. Of particular interest here are the revival of commercial life on 63rd Street, the promotion of modest commercial activity on 61st Street, the reinforcement of commerce on 57th Street to the point of critical mass—including the development of a new "strip" west of Maryland—and the inclusion of commercial activities as a part of the north campus, especially along 55th Street.

BAR

COFFEE SHOP

BOOKSTORE

RESTAURANT

DINING HALL

COMMERCIAL ZONE

Public Motion Study △

Campus Conviviality ▽

■ UNIVERSITY / COMMUNITY GYM	⊞ TENNIS COURTS
■ UNIVERSITY / COMMUNITY POOLS	⊞ BASKETBALL COURTS
■ PARKS	⊡ BASEBALL / PLAYING FIELDS
- - - INTER PARK PATHS	● ● ● GREENLINKS BETWEEN FACILITIES

ATHLETICS

The university currently lacks critical sports facilities and looks to solve its athletic deficit with a very big gym. Without a doubt, the addition of an excellent pool is critical and will be most welcome. The question is where to put it. This plan proposes the space along University Avenue between Bartlett and the Field House with the new facility forming a link between the two. The retention of the Bartlett pool as part of the complex would provide great benefit for non-competitive swimmers and extend these spaces into a sequence potentially reminiscent of the interconnected reading rooms of Harper, replicating the continuous character of the quads, and creating a vivid and focused athletic center.

However, the mentality of the big gym project slights the reality of contemporary physical culture. The national obsession with exercise is extremely diverse and current patterns suggest that, as important as are massive facilities, so is a proliferation of smaller resources, of squash and tennis courts, weight rooms, aerobics studios, and so on. These might be located in smaller gyms—including one on the South Bank, perhaps within the GSB complex—and as components of the expanded commons (Ida Noyes, of course, already has a pool).

While the university is clearly deficient in certain top-drawer athletic facilities, a slightly broader perspective reveals an actual abundance of recreational resources, especially in the park spaces adjoining the campus. Given the differences in rhythm between public and university uses of such facilities, the university might consider strategies for a far more extensive sharing of these spaces, in

The Athletic Archipelago ◁
Natatorium Studies ▽

Washington and Jackson Parks, along the Midway, and on campus. While remaining mindful of the Columbia University crisis of 1968, precipitated by the expansion of university athletic facilities into a public park, it is nevertheless true that the possibility of mutually beneficial cooperation between the university and the community remains.

Such sharing, which could further cement good town/gown relations, would be facilitated by the development of an efficient electronic system of scheduling, and passes to assure fair and convenient access. Such an atmosphere of mutual benefit might also enable far greater flexibility in the location of new facilities. For example, the several derelict repair and storage facilities in Washington Park are candidates to be replaced by athletic fields (a soccer field seems especially needed) to be split between campus and community. Likewise, a modest reconstruction of Stagg Field could supply a fine facility and large-scale gathering space for the university while its shared use by neighborhood high schools would help to create friendly relations between the university and its neighbors. A cross-Midway location for the Business School would offer it a site for its own gym, to be shared with its neighbors. Finally, university participation in the creation of a first-class community gym on 55th Street (enlarging the current one) would take further pressure off of the central facilities.

1 FIELD HOUSE

2 56TH STREET PEDESTRIANIZED

3 BRIDGE OF THIGHS (ABOVE)

4 APPLICANT POOL

5 NATATORIUM

6 OMNIPAIDEUM

7 BARTLETT POOL

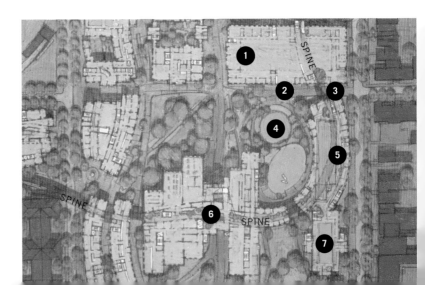

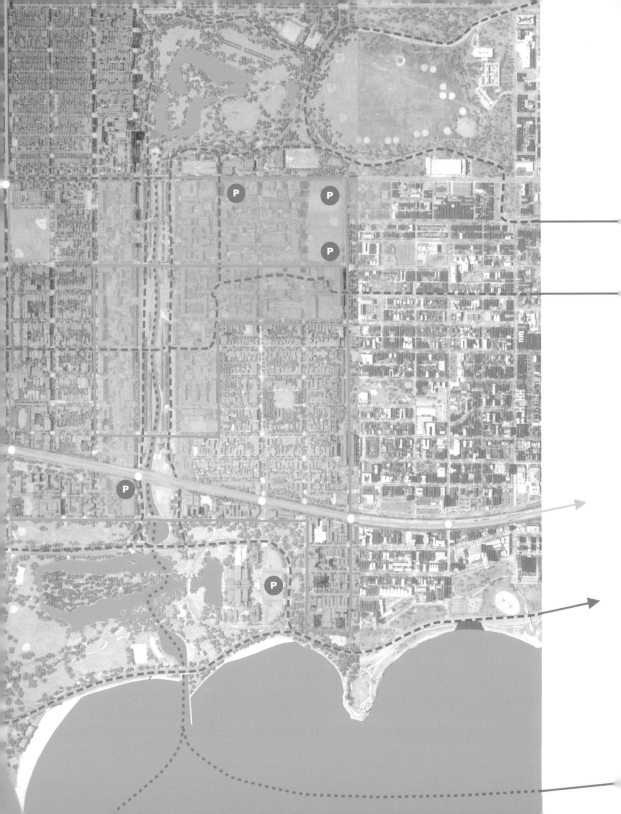

——— CAMPUS BUS		- - - SLO-MO
- - - WATERBORN		▨ PEDESTRIAN CAMPUS
——— METRA		ⓟ PARKING
——— CTA		

MOVEMENT & TRAFFIC

The university campus is a special instance of urban circulation. Unlike most American cities in which the alpha means is the automobile, the campus privileges pedestrians. All decisions about the structure of movement must recognize this priority. To retain this walkable character, every effort must be made to enhance the quality of walking, to relegate the automobile to the campus periphery, to radically slow its movement across campus, to introduce slower, more benign means of movement, and to maximize opportunities for underground storage and building service arrangements.

Traffic, however, is not inevitable. One way of reducing the need for parking is by addressing the demand side of the equation. Clearly, the more members of the university community living in walkable proximity to the campus, the lower the demand for parking facilities. Similarly, increasing the convenience and quality of public transportation will have an effect on demand for parking. The reconstruction of the dingy stations on the METRA line, for example, could have a major impact, especially if relocated to provide direct access to both the north and south campuses. A circulation loop around campus that includes a stop at the 63rd Street El Station would also be helpful. More adventurously, should the Midway become navigable, a fast waterborn service might be instituted to the Gleacher Center and perhaps to Evanston (see pages 68 & 69).

To preserve pedestrianism, parking should be at the campus periphery and conveniently linked both to major access roads and to means of movement to and around the campus. Here the university might innovate technologically, utilizing a slow-speed system conceptually similar to those used for tourist circulation in places like Washington, D.C. To function properly such a system must have an extremely short head time, be very easy to board and leave, and follow a route that conveniently approaches all major campus facilities. An innovatively imagined system would be of a highly non-aggressive design and be environmentally benign.

Parking in this plan is concentrated on two or three major sites with dispersed facilities for the handicapped, for deliveries, and for the privileged. Good locations currently available include the area between the railway embankment and Stony Island Avenue along 60th Street, the enormous area under the athletic fields, and a site near Cottage Grove and 60th Street that might potentially be linked by tunnel to the hospitals. In addition, some shared arrangement with the new lot at the Museum of Science and Industry might be explored as the peak demand times for the university and the museum differ considerably. In any event, parking structures should be avoided in locations of high community value. A lot on 55th Street, for example, will both compromise the quality of that boulevard and destroy the view from dormitories or other campus facilities built nearby. Parking under Stagg, though more expensive than an above-ground structure, is actually the only way of recovering additional value from the athletic fields.

This plan also proposes a new kind of "Slo-Mo" circulation system as part of the development of the campus. This system—lying conceptually between street and pedestrian networks—is predicated on an idea of the compatibility of modes rather than on the traffic engineer's dream of separation. A mix of pedestrians, bikes, and slow-moving, non-polluting vehicles (like the electric carts currently in limited use on campus) would be permitted here. The addition of this system would be, among other things, an acknowledgment of both the large dimensions of the expanded campus and a potential bridge to a neighborhood-wide system.

Movement Study ▷
Slo-Mo Study ▽

EXISTING PARKS   EXISTING QUADS

NEW PARKS   NEW QUADS

YARDS

UNIVERSITY GARDENS

The university sits in the midst of a truly extravagant amount of greenspace, a key to the character both of the campus and its neighborhoods and a crucial connection between them. Two fundamental characteristics describe this greenspace. First is its connectedness, the propagation of parks and quadrangles into a linked system. This can be elaborated both through the creation of new greenspaces and by the reinforcement and re-creation of the links between them via selective inclusion of neighborhood greenways, pedestrianization of streets, and the capture of portions of the system of alleyways for greening and circulation.

Second is the nature of the greenspaces themselves. Inscribed in the urban pattern, these spaces typically have an enclosed, rectilinear character. What's most crucial about these spaces in their campus incarnation, however, is not simply their two-dimensional figurality but their style of creating space, of operating in three dimensions. The relationship of these green spaces to the architecture that encloses them is at the core of their quality. This precisely expressed sense of boundedness and interiority is perhaps the critical issue for their planning and articulation, a sense that the university's current planning treats essentially as an afterthought. Opportunities on north campus, on Stagg Field, along the Midway, and on the west campus to create strong spatial figures are being squandered by a fixation on isolated sites and short-term vision.

The form of the historic campus and its style of reconciliation of greenspace and block form are too good not to continue and too good not to share. The university should energetically promote the spread of the kind of flowing, park-like, figural, pedestrian spaces embodied in the quads as both a system of movement and as the emblematic style of local development. This would not simply add environmental value to surrounding communities, but might also serve as a link, an invitation, to share in the best values of the university community.

The much discussed idea of a botanical garden seems especially germane, both for its didactic and formal character and for introducing the notion that greenspace can and must assume deeper meanings in use. These meanings are found not simply in taxonomic display but also include enlarged possibilities for engaging a sustainable urban ecology, for helping to describe a progressive vision of urban life. Questions of environmental remediation, thermal management, oxygen production, food supply, and so on, are meanings that cement the ties between the university and its surroundings in the most direct possible way.

The university should assume a special role of stewardship not simply for its own quadrangles but for the greening of its surroundings. Such stewardship, in its fundamentally benign character, could become a real bridge between both spaces and people and a fine expression of the university's own sense of citizenship. The abandoned spaces of Woodlawn offer an especially important potential resource, a vast *tabula rasa* between 61st and 63rd Streets. In the short term, these spaces should become green. Community agriculture, nurseries, and street improvements are surely part of the picture. So too is the idea that this moment of physical tractability offers an opportunity to add public infrastructure that can have a long-term effect on community life. The construction of parks, squares, playgrounds, and gardens in anticipation of growth can set the course for a better collective quality of life than piecemeal development and can add value to whatever development ensues. Such green exceptions to the repetitive grid (think of Madison Park) set long-lived patterns of amenity and community.

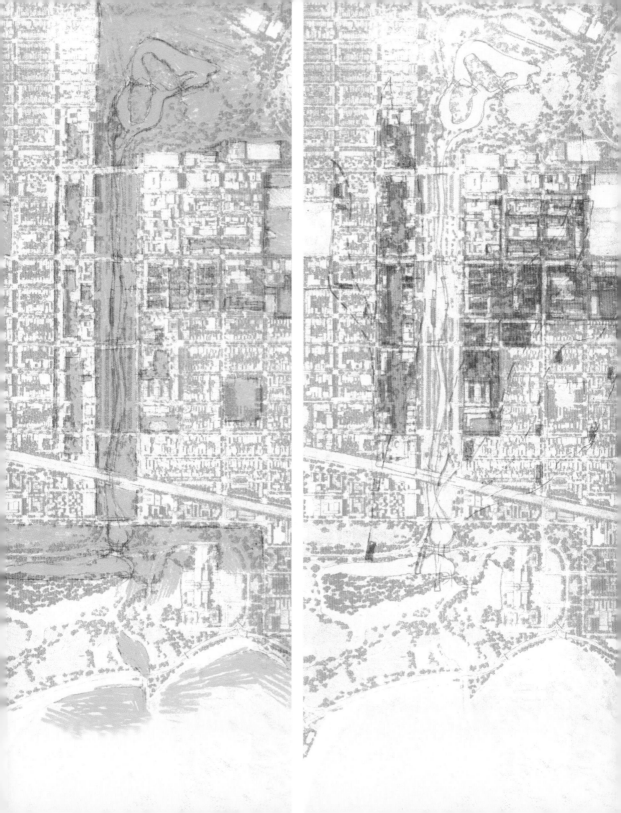

ADDITIVE

The campus is constructed by accretion of elements through a process of lateral layering.

MEGA-STRUCTURAL

The process of addition yields a continuous architectural fabric: *e pluribus unum*. The campus should support, among others, a reading as a single building, built in increments.

LABYRINTHINE

Within the campus mega-structure, numerous alternative routes—both interior and exterior—should be available. One of the pleasures of the labyrinth is the possibility of getting lost.

A: QUALITIES OF QUADS

DISTINCT

A campus is both continuous and discontinuous. The university serves both its own physical and social character and that of its neighborhood by keeping its boundaries clear, beautiful, and porous.

QUADRANGULAR

A quadrangle is a four-sided space: building reinforces its proportion and character. A quadrangle is not simply the landscaping of built elements. Campus architecture is defined by figural spaces, quads, parks, or streets. The limestone mountain range along the Midway is about edge, as are the courts of the old quads.

COMPLEX FORM

Campus buildings should be complex and full of small differences.

NEURAL

The most satisfying metaphor for the university is the subdivided brain. Knowledge has its privileges. Access to the green centers of the Oxbridge quads is honorific, reserved for those with a depth of study.

THICK WALLS

Gothic architecture bears its weight well and visibly. Building walls should mainly be thick. Attention must be given to the balance of opacity and transparency in both individual buildings and in aggregations.

THIN SECTIONS

Building sections too deep risk destroying quadrangular planning forms and excluding daylight. The campus should grow via aggregation, not block-busting.

PEDESTRIANS FIRST

Every addition to the campus must enhance the walking character of its primary spaces. This applies to both horizontal and vertical axes.

First, there is the matter of the master plan. At certain times universities rise to Olympian heights and decide that an overall master plan is necessary, which indeed it is. But far too frequently such a document is treated superficially by the architect, by the administration, and by succeeding architects.

Here is what generally happens. The architect presents the overall plan to the administration. When and if it is accepted in principle and the immediate buildings under consideration are placed and released, the architect then sometimes forgets all about the master plan and concentrates on the current buildings, disregarding their relation to the master plan. The administration generally treats the master plan with similar superficiality, and in many instances forgets all about or ignores its existence. Frequently the only intent of the master plan was for fundraising purposes. The administration often neglects to show an existing master plan and intent to each new architect commissioned to a building, and there is usually very little enthusiasm on the part of new architects to dig up exactly what was intended by earlier studies.

B: THE MASTER PLAN"

Now, these are situations created when there is a master plan. In many instances, colleges and universities have no real master plan. A new building looms on the horizon and the Board of Directors choose to place it themselves. The result of this invention is generally that the best and openest site is decided upon. Not until this decision is reached, is the architect called in. Too often the architect then has to take any responsibility about placing the building, and simply says "yes" to the job. I have even heard of a case where an architect designed a building and told the college officials, "You decide where it should go."

Eero Saarinen, 1960

This summary reflects the recommendations of this plan at the time it was conceived: the implementation of the official plan has rendered many points moot. Nevertheless, as this publication is intended both to record our original ideas as well as to goad the university's thinking in the future, we retain both the fictions of official interest in this work and of its timeliness.

1 PARKING

To maximize pedestrian character while accommodating commuters, the university must build parking structures at the campus perimeter. We do not disagree with this. Our proposal suggests two major new facilities, one underground beneath Stagg Field, large enough to accommodate hospital parking, and another on 60th Street between the rail viaduct and Stony Island Avenue.

C:
POINTS OF
DISAGREEMENT

We believe that the north campus site is unsuitable. Although convenient, it will have a compromising effect on the development of the north campus, degrading its aura and expending a prominent, anchoring site, with potentially excellent views, on a use unable to take advantage of them, ruining the western exposure of the dormitory proposed to its east. For similar reasons we urge the ultimate replacement of the Medical Center parking structure on Cottage Grove and 59th Street which squanders one of the most prominent and potentially engaging sites on campus.

2 HOUSING

We object to the proposed dormitories not for their location but their config-uration. An opportunity has been lost to look at the entire north campus coherently and to join the campus from south to north. The siting of the new dorms both frustrates this flow and compromises the cogency and figuration of the north campus. Indeed, even the possibility of creating quadrangles that carry the spirit of the originals has been lost by the restricted cross-site passage, the understudied interconnection between building elements, and the unsympathetic affect of the architecture of the new dorms.

We also regret the loss of an opportunity to rethink the general character of residential life on campus in a way that exceeds the standard-issue character of the barracks-like dorms. Elsewhere in this study, we urge consideration of a more collegiate or "village" strategy that both expands the possibilities for community residential life and takes greater advantage of the strong character of existing stock. Finally, we wonder at the decision to destroy Woodward Court. Although we are are unaware of its structural condition, the envelope is well-scaled and the existing dining pavilion quite beautiful. Rather than destroying so many perfectly located dorm rooms on a campus desperate for them, further reconsideration of rehabilitation seems logical.

3 THE GRADUATE SCHOOL OF BUSINESS

Not simply do we feel that the existing Saarinen dormitory should remain, we believe its site is too small for the present GSB program and for future needs. This begs the question of expansion and raises the likelihood that Ida Noyes—one of the finest buildings on campus and one with high potential for a greater density of use—will eventually be co-opted for the GSB. This would be a pity given the greater need for residential and commons expansion and the likely growth of the College.

The choice of site also ignores the tremendous opportunities for community and campus synergies should the GSB move to the south campus. A site between 60th and 61st would provide a far more expansive situation for the GSB. It would bring critical mass to a forlorn site and galvanize development. It would also help redress the malign neglect that has characterized the university's relationship to Woodlawn, and, by offering a strong anchor, help to organize Woodlawn's revival.

4 THE INTERDIVISIONAL RESEARCH BUILDING

While the proposed location of the new Interdivisional Research Building is not exactly meretricious, it is unnuanced and sacrifices important possibilities. The demolition of two lovely little historicist buildings—Whitman and the Visual Sciences Building—is by no means trivial and will contribute greatly to the general up-shift of scale in new construction. The site we propose along 56th Street would also entail demolition, but of buildings less architecturally choice.

More important, though, is the foreclosure of important figural options in the planning of the open space of the university. The 56th Street location is predicated on a strategy to maximize figural open space on the campus—as the key armature for architectural organization—by matching building sites with spatial prospects. This location would both provide a strong edge for an expanded set of athletic fields and orient this major building to a great view of those fields, and over them toward the distant Chicago skyline.

5 ELLIS AVENUE

The official plan promotes the importance of Ellis Avenue as the major north-south campus distributor. While there is an argument to be made for this, it derives from the fact that Ellis is the logical *automotive* spine of the campus. The opaque frontages and spare penetrations of most of the buildings along Ellis provide an uncongenial—though not entirely intractable—pedestrian experience, unlikely to be offset by banal "plazas."

The development of an Ellis Avenue spine needs a north-south context. Pedestrian traffic along the considerable distance from 55th to 61st Streets must become congenial if the university is to fully enjoy its bifurcated campus. We suggest a strong axis along what is now the principal north-south pedestrian route on campus: through the center of the main quadrangles. Creating such a purely pedestrian route will require passage through both Regenstein and Harper. These cuts could have strong benefits for the organization and use of both of these buildings as well as a dramatically unifying effect on the campus as a whole.

6 THE GYM

Putting the new gym next to the playing fields seems logical, though the current design provides poor access to those fields, and the main activities housed, swimming and basketball, are not outdoor location-sensitive. The main issue is again the value of the figure of the playing fields to a larger pattern of campus development. In its present location, the new gym precludes the possibility—suggested in this plan—that the east side of Ellis be loaded with arts-related facilities overlooking the sweep of the playing fields and Washington Park beyond, and that a continuous park edge along Stagg and Washington be defined.

We also suggest keeping at least some of Bartlett as a gym, linked, via a new Natatorium, to the Field House and to Regenstein. The advantage would be in the connection between the main campus indoor athletic facilities, the invention of a new quadrangle to the west, and the potential for a continuous sequence of spaces from the Field House to Natatorium to Bartlett to Regenstein to the Science Quads. We also feel that the present plan forces dorm residents to live with views that lack the intimate scale and texture most suitable for private contemplation.

7 THE STYLE FOR THE JOB

For its three initial architectural picks, the university has chosen a cohesive set of practitioners, and not simply in architectural terms. Three elegant Latin Americans whose works sit squarely in the late modernist mainstream represent what is, in many ways, the equivalent of the university's choice of architects at its founding. Drawn from the high-end corporate tier of the profession, none of these architects can be said to represent an adventurous choice. However—given their homogeneous cultural and architectural formations—they do produce a kind of consistency that, in many ways, reproduces the turn-of-the-last-century idea that a variety of practitioners working within a single historical idiom would yield a formula for architectural consistency.

Ironically, though, the settings in which these architects will build are relatively free of the gothic revival architectural context. The gym, dorms, and parking lot are surrounded, for the most part, by greenspace, roadways, and modern buildings of largely indifferent quality. The exception is the powerfully-edged GSB site which, nevertheless, calls for a freestanding complex that must mediate between strong gothic and modern buildings. The loss to the university is of sites that might have supported bolder choices.

8 THE VALUE OF THE FIGURAL GROUND

The deductive style of the university's planning process treats the quality of landscape as subsidiary to issues of organization and construction. The process proceeds from programming to diagram to building and, finally, to landscaping. Plazas along Ellis, residual spaces behind a parking lot, an over-scaled patch on the Science Quad, unspecified modifications to the Midway landscape, an unnecessary ornamental gateway on the Main Quads—the plan tenders only emotionless, bean-counting suggestions, without aspiration, focused not on a setting for the life of the mind but on parking slots and a spurious style of spatial efficiency. The university's magnificent architectural and landscape heritage seems meaningless to its planners, whose planning tactics are trivial and whose architectural sensibility is an embarrassment.

New York's Central Park—whose spirit is richly present in the university's own Olmstedean borders—is the classic example of a landscape space that creates the character of its own architectural boundaries, a quad on steroids. Designed and executed before the city grew to meet it, Central Park created a powerful condition at its edges and invented a receptive architectural typology to permit its neighbors to enjoy it. The campus has a double opportunity to create an architecture in relationship to open space. Both long ranges of sites along actual Omstedean parks and their miniature versions on the interiors of the quads offer the chance for buildings to be doubly directed, a truly inspirational condition.

9 THE MULTIPLICATION OF LINKS

It is striking that all of the new projects proposed for the campus are freestanding buildings. Much of the genius of the original quadrangles—as of the Oxbridge paradigm that inspired them—grows out of tight proximity and frequent connection between buildings. The official plan dissipates the sense of labyrinth, in its failures to connect and in its assumption that a big program must inevitably create a big building.

The university's planners are out of touch not only with the historic character of the best of the university's spaces and with their precedents but with the architectural practices that have, in recent years, focused on strategies of assembly, of management of scale, and of combinatory effects. A strategy focused on creating spaces and structures of greater intimacy, intricacy, and connectivity is critical to retaining a sense of scale and complexity that will be overwhelmed should current scale-creep persist unabated.

10 THE NEIGHBORHOOD

The university's plan takes only a slight interest in its surrounding neighborhoods, gun-shy, perhaps, about the appearance of intrusion. Steps to create better relations to the south—where neighborhood victimization remains most graphic—are suggested elsewhere. It is also time, however, to reexamine some of the worst outcomes of the "successful" urban renewal schemes of the fifties and sixties, to attempt to restore the sense of street life obliterated by those devastating plans.

Perhaps the worst casualty is 55th Street, which remains virtually dead. The official plan makes a modest beginning to return some conviviality to it by placing commercial space on a portion of the ground floor of its new garage (although the garage itself can hardly be called helpful). This should be maximally extended. Candidates for replacement include the bizarre berms on the north side of the street, the dreadful one-story brick bunkers for the elderly east of Woodlawn, several parking lots, and a portion of the south edge of Kimbark Park.

Also crucial to the restoration of life to the neighborhood is the scrupulous enhancement of 57th Street. Elsewhere, we identify the potential of this street as a neighborhood cultural spine and we encourage the effort to incorporate additional commercial space both to the east of Woodlawn and to the west of Ellis. The latter is especially vital as the university continues its growth in that direction, creating a community that will be increasingly underserved. A number of sites are available, including the ground floor of the Interdivisional Research Building, the ground floor of the DCAM parking lot, the block opposite it, and the frontage along Cottage Grove.

11 THE MIDWAY

Like the rest of the university master plan, proposals for the Midway represent a compromise at best. To be sure, the addition of a skating rink, the reconstruction of street crossings into fake bridges, and the relandscaping of the side panels of the Midway to serve as gardens and playing fields represent a net gain in quality. All, however, offer more of an ornamental than a structural approach. Although it is only a block wide, the Midway holds no fewer than four east-west streets along its length and its greenspaces remain, in many ways, accessory to its function as a circulation artery.

We suggest combining the two center roads with 60th Street to create a boulevard along the south side of the Midway. Freeing the entire space of traffic would permit more dramatic treatment of its interior and we propose—elaborating on Olmsted's original plan—a waterway linking Washington and Jackson Parks. This would not simply render the space remarkable, it would yield a truly useful and magnetic park and a grand unifier of the split campus, the biggest quad.

12 THE SOUTH CAMPUS

As this plan finally goes to press, we learn that the university has commissioned its original planner to prepare a plan for the south campus. We hope it is a good one but are skeptical and chagrined by a decision to extend the contract of planners so demonstrably dull. We have learned that one of the principal suggestions of the south campus plan is for a deep set-back along 61st Street. Again, this is a suggestion that, in and of itself, is neither here nor there, demanding the validation of architecture to prove its quality.

Creating another front face for the campus is logical, even critical. In the abstract, an equally compelling case could surely be made for maintaining the street wall, for arcades, or for a truly deep and usable green face, oriented south and shared with the Woodlawn community.

What is needed is a strong conceptual and architectural plan. We have proposed organizing the south campus into three lateral quadrangles; moving the GSB south to provide major leverage, building new commons and residential spaces, assuring a continuous building frontage along 61st Street, constructing figural park space within Woodlawn, and rallying strong efforts to revive 63rd Street as a commercial corridor. Although we do not feel that the university has a manifest destiny to further expand into Woodlawn—quite the opposite—we do feel that the university serves itself, and its community, by acting with exemplary and generous neighborliness.

PROJECT PREPARED BY THE MICHAEL SORKIN STUDIO

MICHAEL SORKIN AND ANDREI VOVK, PARTNERS

ACKNOWLEDGMENTS   PROJECT TEAM:

MICHAEL CARSTENS
THERESA HIMMER
MITCHELL JOACHIM
JACOB KAIN
VICTORIA MARSHALL
JONATHAN SOLOMON
SHIRLEY TING
YUKIKO YOKOO

SPECIAL THANKS:

RICHARD BUMSTEAD
KATHERINE FISCHER TAYLOR
MAX GRINNELL '98
ANDREW YANG '01

In memory of Dale Good